Meet America's Presidents!

2-Minute visits

Scott Peters

The Presidents

George Washington	p.2	Benjamin Harrison	p.24
John Adams	p.3	William McKinley	p.25
Thomas Jefferson	p.4	Theodore Roosevelt	p.26
James Madison	p.5	William Howard Taft	p.27
James Monroe	p.6	Woodrow Wilson	p.28
John Quincy Adams	p.7	Warren Harding	p.29
Andrew Jackson	p.8	Calvin Coolidge	p.30
Martin Van Buren	p.9	Herbert Hoover	p.31
William Henry Harrison	p.10	Franklin D Roosevelt	p.32
John Tyler	p.11	Harry Truman	p.33
James Polk	p.12	Dwight d Eisenhower	p.34
Zachary Taylor	p.13	John F Kennedy	p.35
Millard Fillmore	p.14	Lyndon B Johnson	p.36
Franklin Pierce	p.15	Richard Nixon	p.38
James Buchanan	p.16	Gerald Ford	p.39
Abraham Lincoln	p.17	Jimmy Carter	p.40
Andrew Johnson	p.18	Ronald Reagan	p.41
Ulysses S Grant	p.19	George Bush	p.42
Rutherford Hayes	p.20	Bill Clinton	p.43
James Garfield	p.21	George W Bush	p.44
Chester Arthur	p.22	Barack Obama	p.45
Grover Cleveland	p.23	Donald Trump	p.46

GEORGE WASHINGTON
1ST

1789 TO 1797

HOW HE'S REMEMBERED

The "Father of His Country", George Washington was America's First President.

He used the newly written Constitution to build the government, creating many roles and traditions that are still used today.

His face appears on the US dollar bill and quarter.

BORN:
Feb 22, 1732
Westmoreland County, Virginia

DIED:
Dec 14, 1799
Mount Vernon, Virginia
after a brief illness

STRANGE & FASCINATING FACTS

According to rumor, George Washington had wooden teeth. In actual fact, his dentures were made of animal teeth, lead, brass screws, gold wire, hippopotamus ivory, and even bone!

He had no middle name.

He stepped down from office after 8 years because he felt strongly that the president is not a king.

No one will ever outrank him in the military.

"Associate yourself with men of good quality if you esteem your own reputation; for 'tis better to be alone than in bad company."
- George Washington

First US President

Of Terms: 2

Party: Unaffiliated

JOHN ADAMS

2ND

1797 to 1801

HOW HE'S REMEMBERED

Before becoming president, he was America's very first vice president.

He helped create the Declaration of Independence, and was one of only two people who signed it.

He forged peace with France to help end the American Revolutionary War.

Born:
Oct 30, 1735
Quincy, Massachusetts

Died:
Jul 4, 1826
Quincy, Massachusetts
of heart failure

STRANGE & FASCINATING FACTS

John Adams traveled to England and visited William Shakespeare's birthplace. While there, he carved off a piece of one of the famous playwright's chairs as a souvenir.

He was the very first president to live in the White House.

His nickname was His Rotundity because he was overweight.

He was a great pen pal.

"To be good, and to do good, is all we have to do."
- John Adams

Second US President

Of Terms: 1

Party: Federalist

THOMAS JEFFERSON
3RD

1801 to 1809

HOW HE'S REMEMBERED

A founding father, he helped write the Declaration of Independence.

He made the Louisiana Purchase, doubling the size of the country.

He hired Lewis and Clark to explore the new western territory and report back.

He lowered taxes.

Born:
Apr 13, 1743
Albemarle County, Virginia

Died:
Jul 4, 1826
Albemarle County, Virginia
of pneumonia and kidney infection

STRANGE & FASCINATING FACTS

He enjoyed meteorology and kept detailed daily records of the weather.

He had a pet mockingbird.

He loved books and owned nearly 6000 volumes!

His huge book collection became the start of the Library of Congress.

He once shocked people by eating a tomato.

"Nothing can stop the man with the right mental attitude from achieving his goal; nothing on earth can help the man with the wrong mental attitude."
- Thomas Jefferson

Third US President
Of Terms: 2
Party: Democratic-Republican

JAMES MADISON

4TH

1809 to 1817

HOW HE'S REMEMBERED

He helped create both the Constitution and the Bill of Rights.

He presided over the War of 1812, a conflict between the US and England.

During the war, the British burned down the White House. However, his forces won the final battle.

Born:
Mar 16, 1751
Port Conway, Virginia

Died:
Jun 28, 1836
Montpelier, Virginia
of heart failure

STRANGE & FASCINATING FACTS

Madison was 5 feet 4 inches tall and weighed only 100 pounds.

His last words were, "I talk better lying down."

His wife Dolley saved a portrait of George Washington when the British set fire to the White House.

Madison and George Washington are the only two presidents who signed the Constitution.

"The circulation of confidence is better than the circulation of money."
- James Madison

Fourth US President
Of Terms: 2
Party: Democratic-Republican

JAMES MONROE

5TH

1817 to 1825

HOW HE'S REMEMBERED

James Monroe created the Monroe Doctrine. It told European countries that they could no longer try to control America or colonize American land.

Five states were added to the US during his presidency: Mississippi, Illinois, Maine, Alabama, and Missouri.

Born:
Apr 28, 1758
Westmoreland County, Virginia

Died:
Jul 4, 1831
New York, New York
of tuberculosis

STRANGE & FASCINATING FACTS

James Monroe initially opposed the constitution.

He was shot in the shoulder at the battle of Trenton.

As a special envoy, Monroe rode a donkey from Paris, France to Madrid, Spain to try and convince Spain to give what's now Florida to the US.

He was the third president to die on the 4th of July, Independence Day.

"Our country may be likened to a new house. We lack many things, but we possess the most precious of all—liberty!"
- James Monroe

Fifth US President

Of Terms: 2

Party: Democratic-Republican

6

JOHN QUINCY ADAMS

6TH

1825 to 1829

HOW HE'S REMEMBERED

Before becoming president, Adams purchased Florida from Spain for just $5 million when he was secretary of state.

He tried to build a network of roads canals to help connect a growing nation, but it failed in Congress.

He encouraged the advancement of science.

Born:
Jul 11, 1767
Braintree, Massachusetts

Died:
Feb 23, 1848
Washington, DC
of a stroke

STRANGE & FASCINATING FACTS

John Quincy Adams kept a pet alligator in the White House bathtub.

He skinny-dipped in the Potomac River and, while swimming, a female gossip columnist sat on his clothes. She wouldn't give them back until he agreed to an interview.

He became a lawyer without going to law school.

"If your actions inspire others to dream more, learn more, do more and become more, you are a leader."
- John Quincy Adams

Sixth US President
Of Terms: 1
Party: Democratic Republican

ANDREW JACKSON
7TH

1829 to 1837

HOW HE'S REMEMBERED

As a war general, Andrew Jackson beat the British in the final deciding battle for America's independence: The Battle of Orleans.

He formed the Democratic Party, creating the two-party system that's still used today.

He was the first 'common man' to become president.

Born: Mar 15, 1767 Waxhaws Region

Died: Jun 8, 1845 Hermitage (Nashville), Tennessee of heart failure

STRANGE & FASCINATING FACTS

When he was 13, Andrew Jackson Became a messenger for the local militia during the Revolutionary War.

He killed a man who insulted his wife, Rachel. The two men dueled and Jackson won.

He often got into fights and was known for being violent.

He won the popular vote for president three times.

"Any man worth his salt will stick up for what he believes right, but it takes a slightly better man to acknowledge instantly and without reservation that he is in error."
- Andrew Jackson

Seventh US President

Of Terms: 2

Party: Democrtic

MARTIN VAN BUREN

8TH

1837 to 1841

HOW HE'S REMEMBERED

He refused to allow Texas to become a state.

The stock market suffered a terrible crash during his presidency, earning him the nickname Martin Van Ruin.

Cherokee Indians were marched across country and many thousands died in what's known as the Trail of Tears.

Born:
Dec 5, 1782
Kinderhook, New York

Died:
Jul 24, 1862
Kinderhook, New York
of asthma

STRANGE & FASCINATING FACTS

He was the first president born as a US citizen. Previous presidents were British citizens.

Martin Van Buren popularized the phrase OK. Born in Kinderhook, his nickname was Old Kinderhook. During his campaign rallies, his supporters shortened it to "OK".

His first language was Dutch.

He wasn't formally educated until he was 14.

"It is easier to do a job right than to explain why you didn't."
- Martin Van Buren

Eighth US President
Of Terms: 1
Party: Democrat

9TH WILLIAM HENRY HARRISON

1841

HOW HE'S REMEMBERED

Before his presidency, he served as secretary of the Northwest Territory. He developed the Harrison Land Act, which let people buy smaller plots of land. This meant more people could afford to own land.

He only served for one month, and was the first president to die in office.

Born:
Feb 9, 1773
Charles City County, Virginia

Died:
Apr 4, 1841
Washington, DC
of typhoid fever

STRANGE & FASCINATING FACTS

William Henry Harrison gave the longest inauguration speech to date. It clocked in at an hour and a half (compared to the usual 30-60 minute speech). It was outside and the weather was horrible. He got sick afterward and died around a month later.

His grandson became the 23rd United States President.

"Times change, and we change with them."
- William Henry Harrison

Ninth US President
Of Terms: 1 Partial
Party: Whig

JOHN TYLER

10TH

1841 to 1845

HOW HE'S REMEMBERED

John Tyler was the first vice president to take over as president when the elected president died in office.

Instead of setting one law about slavery for the whole country, he told each state to set their own law. So slavery was legal in some states but not in others.

This may have helped cause the Civil War.

Born:
Mar 29, 1790
Charles City County, Virginia

Died:
Jan 18, 1862
Richmond, Virginia
of a stroke

STRANGE & FASCINATING FACTS

John Tyler was born 230 years ago in 1790 but has two living grandkids! As of 2020, they are Lyon Gardiner Tyler Jr. and Harrison Ruffin Tyler, born in 1924 and 1928.

He was nicknamed His Accidency as his rivals said he was nominated by accident.

Why? He went from vice president to president when William Henry Harrison died just a month into his term.

"I can never consent to being dictated to."
- John Tyler

Tenth US President
Of Terms: 1 Partial
Party: Whig

11TH

JAMES POLK

1845 to 1849

HOW HE'S REMEMBERED

He added 1.2 square miles to the United States, making it stretch from the East to the West Coast via the treaty of Guadalupe Hidalgo.

Institutions begun during his office are:
- The Smithsonian Museum
- The US Naval Academy.

Also, the first postage stamps were issued.

Born:
Nov 2, 1795
Mecklenburg County, North Carolina

Died:
Jun 15, 1849
Nashville, Tennessee
of cholera

STRANGE & FASCINATING FACTS

James Polk and his wife were anti-fun. They banned all types of fun from the White House, including dancing and card playing.

He was a sickly child and had his gallstones surgically removed with no painkillers at all!

He was the first president to have his photo taken while in office.

His nickname was Young Hickory.

"The gratitude should be commensurate with the boundless blessings which we enjoy."
- James Polk

Eleventh US President
Of Terms: 1
Party: Democrat

ZACHARY TAYLOR
12TH

1849 to 1850

HOW HE'S REMEMBERED

Despite being a slaveholder, he set the stage for abolition.

He angered slavery supporters when he stood up against slavery, and the country moved toward civil war.

He grew up on the American frontier and was known for his homespun ways.

Born:
Nov 24, 1784
Orange County, Virginia

Died:
Jul 9, 1850
Washington, DC
of gastroenteritis

STRANGE & FASCINATING FACTS

His nickname was Old Rough and Ready.

Growing up, he lived in a log cabin.

He died from eating a bad batch of buttermilk and cherries. Some say he was poisoned!

600 Indians set fire to Taylor's camp during the War of 1812. Taylor and 15 men leaped into action. They doused the blaze before the flames trapped them.

"I have always done my duty. I am ready to die. My only regret is for the friends I leave behind me."
- Zachary Taylor

Twelfth US President

Of Terms: 1 Partial

Party: Whig

13TH MILLARD FILLMORE

1850 to 1853

HOW HE'S REMEMBERED

Fillmore tried to establish the Compromise of 1850 to create peace between the North and the South regarding slavery and abolition.

He expanded US trade into countries in the Far East.

He stopped France from taking over the Hawaiian Islands.

Born:
Jan 7, 1800
Cayuga County, New York

Died:
Mar 8, 1874
Buffalo, New York
of a stroke

STRANGE & FASCINATING FACTS

Fillmore had no vice president! He served without one because he rose from vice president to President himself when President Taylor died in office. There were no rules yet about how to handle this difficulty. In fact, that didn't happen until 1967.

He fell in love with his teacher and married her.

During the civil war, he opposed Abraham Lincoln.

"An honorable defeat is better than a dishonorable victory."
- Millard Fillmore

Thirteenth US President
Of Terms: 1 Partial
Party: Whig

FRANKLIN PIERCE
14TH
1853 to 1857

HOW HE'S REMEMBERED

A murky legacy, Franklin Pierce openly advocated for pro-slavery states in the 1850s. This attitude may have pushed America into Civil War.

He purchased the land that is now New Mexico and Arizona for just $10 million.

Born:
Nov 23, 1804
Hillsborough, New Hampshire

Died:
Oct 8, 1869
Concord, New Hampshire
of liver disease

STRANGE & FASCINATING FACTS

Police arrested him for running over a woman with his horse. However, they didn't have enough evidence to send him to jail.

He perfected the comb-over.

He was friends with the writers Nathaniel Hawthorne and Henry Wadsworth Longfellow.

He was the first president to hire a bodyguard (he was unpopular).

"While men inhabiting different parts of this vast continent cannot be expected to hold the same opinions, they can unite in a common objective and sustain common principles."
- Franklin Pierce

Fourteenth US President
Of Terms: 1
Party: Democrat

JAMES BUCHANAN
15TH

1857 to 1861

HOW HE'S REMEMBERED

James Buchanan claimed to be against slavery, but he refused to support abolition.

He stood behind the Supreme Court's Dred Scott ruling that said the government had no right to stop slavery.

The Civil War began. Several states left or 'seceded' from the Union, and he did nothing to stop them.

Born:
Apr 23, 1791
near Cove Gap,
Pennsylvania

Died:
Jun 1, 1868
Lancaster, Pennsylvania
of respiratory failure

STRANGE & FASCINATING FACTS

Buchanan's childhood home was turned into a hotel called the James Buchanan Hotel.

People often called him doughface because he was from the north but favored southern opinions. Doughface meant you could be molded like dough or clay, meaning people could tell you what to think.

He was the only president who never married.

"The test of leadership is not to put greatness into humanity, but to elicit it, for the greatness is already there."
- James Buchanan

Fifteenth US President

Of Terms: 1

Party: Democrat

ABRAHAM LINCOLN
16TH

1861 to 1865

HOW HE'S REMEMBERED

He led the country during the Civil War, fighting to keep the country united while ending slavery.

He signed the Emancipation Proclamation that freed the slaves and set the United States on a path toward becoming free and equal.

He was murdered just one month into his presidency.

Born:
Feb 12, 1809
LaRue County, Kentucky

Died:
Apr 15, 1865
Washington, DC
of a gunshot wound

STRANGE & FASCINATING FACTS

Abraham Lincoln won every wrestling match he fought except one.

He established Thanksgiving as a national holiday.

He dreamed he'd be assassinated the night before it happened.

He wanted women to have the vote in 1836.

He liked to tell jokes.

"Four score and seven years ago our fathers brought forth on this continent, a new nation, conceived in Liberty, and dedicated to the proposition that all men are created equal."
- Abraham Lincoln

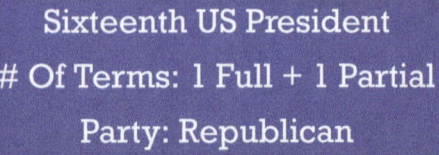

Sixteenth US President
Of Terms: 1 Full + 1 Partial
Party: Republican

ANDREW JOHNSON

17TH

1865 to 1869

HOW HE'S REMEMBERED

He took over after Lincoln was assassinated.

He became known as the Veto President because he blocked so many bills. People felt he was abusing his power.

He often sided with the South.

He was the first president to be impeached.

Born:
Dec 29, 1808
Raleigh, North Carolina

Died:
Jul 31, 1875
near Elizabethton,
Tennessee of a stroke

STRANGE & FASCINATING FACTS

As a child, Andrew Johnson was an indentured servant for two years.

As a servant, he learned to sew and as president, he sewed many of his own suits.

He took care of a family of mice.

He never went to school.

He once suggested that God had Lincoln killed so he could become president.

"If you always support the correct principles then you will never get the wrong results!"
- Andrew Johnson

Seventeenth US President

Of Terms: 1 Partial

Party: Union

ULYSSES S GRANT

18TH

1869 to 1877

HOW HE'S REMEMBERED

He championed the rights of freed slaves, giving black men the right to vote.

A war hero during the Civil War, Grant led the Union troops against the Confederate Army and won.

He created both the National Park System and the Department of Justice.

Born:
Apr 27, 1822
Point Pleasant, Ohio

Died:
July 23, 1885
Wilton, New York
of throat cancer

STRANGE & FASCINATING FACTS

He hated wearing army uniforms.

At his inaugural ball, a bunch of canary birds brought in to brighten up the party froze to death.

On the night Lincoln was assassinated, Grant was supposed to be with him at the theater.

The letter S in his name didn't stand for anything.

"In every battle there comes a time when both sides consider themselves beaten, then he who continues the attack wins."
- Ulysses S Grant

Eighteenth US President

Of Terms: 2

Party: Republican

19TH
RUTHERFORD B HAYES

1877 to 1881

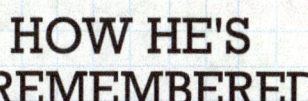

HOW HE'S REMEMBERED

Hayes lost the popular vote, but won after a famous fight between the two parties. Some say he cheated.

He worked to improve the government and create rights protections for all citizens.

He presided over the rebuilding in the South after the destruction caused by the Civil War.

Born:
Oct 4, 1822
Delaware, Ohio

Died:
Jan 17, 1893
Fremont, Ohio
of heart disease

STRANGE & FASCINATING FACTS

Hayes held the first Easter egg roll on the White House lawn.

He said he'd only serve one presidential term, and he kept that promise.

He never served alcohol in the White House. His wife served lemonade instead, so people called her Lemonade Lucy.

The letter 'B' for his middle name stands for Birchard.

"Every expert was once a beginner."
- Rutherford B Hayes

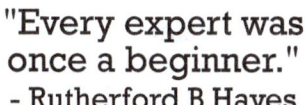

Nineteenth US President

Of Terms: 1

Party: Republican

20

JAMES GARFIELD
20TH

1881

HOW HE'S REMEMBERED

He was assassinated after just 200 days in office. The man who killed him was angry at Garfield because he refused to give him a job in his administration.

While in office, he tried to root out political corruption. He refused to hire people as political favors. He felt the best qualified people should get the jobs.

Born:
Nov 19, 1831
Cuyahoga County, Ohio

Died:
Sept 19, 1881
Elberon, New Jersey
of a gunshot wound

STRANGE & FASCINATING FACTS

He was known as the preacher president because he had a strong, powerful voice.

Garfield could write in two different languages at one time.

He loved adventure novels and originally wanted to become a sailor on the open seas.

He invented the first air conditioner.

"Right reason is stronger than force."
- James Garfield

Twentieth US President
Of Terms: 1 Partial
Party: Republican

21ST CHESTER ARTHUR

1881 to 1885

HOW HE'S REMEMBERED

Arthur became president because Garfield was shot.

He expanded the navy with new ships.

He improved educational opportunities for Native Americans.

The Pendleton Act was created was to give out jobs to qualified people instead of as favors.

Born:
Oct 5, 1829
Fairfield, Vermont

Died:
Nov 18, 1886
New York, New York
of a stroke

STRANGE & FASCINATING FACTS

Chester Arthur sold off a ton of priceless presidential artifacts, including a pair of Lincoln's pants, so that he could pay to redecorate the White House.

Speaking of pants, Arthur loved them and owned over 80 pairs.

Some say he was born in Ireland or Canada, not the US.

He loved fishing.

"Be fit for more than the thing you are now doing. Let everyone know that you have a reserve in yourself; that you have more power than you are now using."
- Chester Arthur

Twenty-First US President
Of Terms: 1 Partial
Party: Republican

GROVER CLEVELAND

22ND AND 24TH

1885-1889 & 1893-1897

HOW HE'S REMEMBERED

He's the only president to serve two terms that were NOT back-to-back, meaning he served one term, lost the following election, and then won again.

Unfortunately, the economy cratered during his second term.

He's the only president to be married at the White House.

Born:
Mar 18, 1837
Caldwell, New Jersey

Died:
Jun 24, 1908
Princeton, New Jersey
of a heart attack

STRANGE & FASCINATING FACTS

Grover Cleveland married his adopted daughter when she was 21 and he was 48.
She was the youngest First Lady.

The Baby Ruth chocolate bar was named after his daughter, Ruth—not the baseball player, Babe Ruth.

He paid a man $150 to fight in his place during the Civil War.

He was the first president to be filmed.

"It is better to be defeated standing for a high principle than to run by committing subterfuge."
- Grover Cleveland

22nd and 24th US President

Of Terms: 2

Party: Democrat

23RD
BENJAMIN HARRISON

1889 to 1893

HOW HE'S REMEMBERED

He grew the federal budget to over $1 billion and spent it on the navy and US coastal harbors.

He added 6 states: Idaho, Washington, Montana, North and South Dakota, and Wyoming.

He signed the Sherman Anti-Trust Act that protects consumers from monopolies and cartels.

Born:
Aug 20, 1833
North Bend, Ohio

Died:
Mar 13, 1901
Indianapolis, Indiana
of pneumonia

STRANGE & FASCINATING FACTS

Benjamin Harrison refused to touch light switches because he was terrified he'd get electrocuted.

However, he was the first president to have electricity in the White House!

His personality was so stiff, people called him the human iceberg.

He was the first president whose voice was recorded.

"Great lives never go out;
they go on."
- Benjamin Harrison

Twenty-Third US President

Of Terms: 1

Party: Republican

WILLIAM McKINLEY
25TH

1897 to 1901

HOW HE'S REMEMBERED

McKinley was president during the Spanish-American war. He wanted to make America a world power.

An imperialist, McKinley brought these territories under American control: Guam, Hawaii, Puerto Rico, and the Philippines.

He began the building of the Panama Canal.

Born:
Jan 29, 1843
Niles, Ohio

Died:
Sept 14, 1901
Buffalo, New York
of gangrene from a gunshot wound

STRANGE & FASCINATING FACTS

William McKinley had a parrot named Washington Post.

He loved fishing, horseback riding, and swimming.

He was the first president to ride in an automobile.

His face is on the $500 bill.

McKinley removed his good luck charm, a red carnation, to give it to a little girl. He was shot shortly afterward.

"In the time of darkest defeat, victory may be nearest."
- William McKinley

Twenty-Fifth US President
Of Terms: 1 Full + 1 Partial
Party: Republican

THEODORE ROOSEVELT
26TH

1901 to 1909

HOW HE'S REMEMBERED

The youngest president at 42, his charisma made the office popular once again.

He increased food and drug safety standards.

He expanded national forests and lands.

His 'Big Stick Diplomacy' stated that the US would protect other countries under threat.

Born:
Oct 27, 1858
New York, New York

Died:
Jan 6, 1919
Oyster Bay, New York
of a heart attack

"Speak softly and carry a big stick."
- Theodore Roosevelt

Twenty-Sixth US President
Of Terms: 1 Full + 1 Partial
Party: Republican

STRANGE & FASCINATING FACTS

Every member of his family owned stilts—even the First Lady!

He was shot while giving a speech, kept talking, and lived.

He was an avid boxer, but after a boxing fight in the White House blinded him in one eye, he switched to jiu-jitsu instead.

He was the father of the US Navy.

He was the first president to win a Nobel Peace Prize.

WILLIAM HOWARD TAFT

27TH

1909 to 1913

HOW HE'S REMEMBERED

William Howard Taft set up the US parcel post service.

He created the federal income tax via the 16th amendment.

He was the only president to also serve as Supreme Court Chief Justice (8 years after the end of his term).

Arizona and New Mexico states were added.

Born:
Sept 15, 1857
Cincinnati, Ohio

Died:
Mar 8, 1930
Washington, DC
of heart disease

STRANGE & FASCINATING FACTS

He was a very large man, and according to rumor he once got stuck the White House bath tub!

Once during a parade in his honor, he fell asleep.

He was a wrestling champion. As a kid, he was good at baseball.

After his time in office, he lost 80 pounds.

"We must dare to be great; and we must realize that greatness is the fruit of toil and sacrifice and high courage."
- William Howard Taft

Twenty-Seventh US President

Of Terms: 1

Party: Republican

WOODROW WILSON
28TH

1913 to 1921

HOW HE'S REMEMBERED

Woodrow Wilson created the Federal Reserve system, which helps protect America's money supply.

He started the sliding scale tax system so that people who earn less pay less than the rich.

He brought the US into World War I, after campaigning on the promise that he'd keep the US out of it.

Born:
Dec 28, 1856
Staunton, Virginia

Died:
Feb 3, 1924
Washington, DC
of a stroke

STRANGE & FASCINATING FACTS

He painted his golf balls black during the winter so that he could find them in the snow.

He's the only president buried in Washington, DC.

As a child, he struggled with dyslexia in school, but he worked hard and became an excellent student.

His face is on the $100,000 bill.

"The object of love is to serve, not to win."
- Woodrow Wilson

Twenty-Eighth US President
Of Terms: 2
Party: Democrat

29TH
WARREN HARDING
1921 to 1923

HOW HE'S REMEMBERED

He signed the treaty that ended US involvement in World War I.

However, he was known as one of America's worst presidents. He was involved in many scandals. One was the Teapot Scandal, where public oil reserves were sold off in secret to line crooks' pockets with money.

Born:
Nov 2, 1865
Morrow County, Ohio

Died:
Aug 2, 1923
San Francisco, California
of congestive heart failure

STRANGE & FASCINATING FACTS

Harding was the first president to talk on the radio.

He had huge feet—size 19—the largest in presidential history.

He started a newspaper before becoming president.

As a kid, his nickname was Winnie.

He met his wife, Florence, when she was teaching his sister to play piano.

"There's good in everybody. Boost. Don't knock."
- Warren Harding

Twenty-Ninth US President
Of Terms: 1 Partial
Party: Republican

30TH CALVIN COOLIDGE

1923 to 1929

HOW HE'S REMEMBERED

Calvin Coolidge cleaned up the corruption mess that President Harding left behind.

America prospered under Coolidge and the times were called The Roaring Twenties.

He signed the Indian Citizenship Act, giving full citizenship to all Native Americans.

Born:
Jul 4, 1872
Plymouth, Vermont

Died:
Jan 5, 1933
Northampton, Massachusetts
of a heart attack

STRANGE & FASCINATING FACTS

Calvin Coolidge is the only president born on the 4th of July.

His own father swore him into office in the middle of the night when President Harding died unexpectedly.

He had two pet raccoons named Reuben and Rebecca.

According to rumor, he liked having his scalp massaged with petroleum jelly while he ate breakfast in bed.

"If you see ten troubles coming down the road, you can be sure that nine will run into the ditch before they reach you."
- Calvin Coolidge

Thirtieth US President
Of Terms: 1 Full + 1 Partial
Party: Republican

HERBERT HOOVER

31ST

1929 to 1933

HOW HE'S REMEMBERED

He presided over the Great Depression, for which he took much blame.

He paved the way for airplane safety by introducing the Federal Aviation Administration.

He signed the order to make the Star Spangled Banner the national anthem.

Born:
Aug 10, 1874
West Branch, Iowa

Died:
Oct 20, 1964
New York, New York
of internal bleeding

STRANGE & FASCINATING FACTS

He was orphaned when he was 9.

Hoover and his wife had a special way to stop people from snooping on their conversations: they spoke Mandarin Chinese.

He once pushed ore carts at a gold mine in California.

He helped feed World War I refugees.

He took part in the first long-distance TV broadcast.

"Be patient and calm; no one can catch a fish with anger."
- Herbert Hoover

Thirty-First US President
Of Terms: 1
Party: Republican

32ND FRANKLIN D ROOSEVELT

1933 to 1945

HOW HE'S REMEMBERED

He successfully led America out of the Great Depression and back to prosperity.

He created the Social Security program.

He brought the US into World War II.

He's the only president to serve more than 2 terms—in fact, he was elected to serve 4 terms.

Born:
Jan 30, 1882
Hyde Park, New York

Died:
Apr 12, 1945
Warm Springs, Georgia
of a stroke

STRANGE & FASCINATING FACTS

He was the first president to fly in a plane.

He was a distant relative of both his wife and 10 other presidents.

He loved stamp collecting.

Polio disease left his legs crippled, but he tried hard to hide the fact.

During World War II, he spoke to Americans through his radio broadcast "fireside chats".

"Men are not prisoners of fate, but only prisoners of their own minds."
- Franklin D Roosevelt

Thirty-Second US President
Of Terms: 3 Full + 1 Partial
Party: Democrat

33RD

HARRY S TRUMAN

1945 to 1953

HOW HE'S REMEMBERED

Truman made the decision to drop the atomic bomb on Japan to bring an end to World War II.

He presided over the beginning of the Cold War with Russia, and helped form NATO (the North Atlantic Treaty Organization) with Canada and Western Europe. They agreed to fend off Russia together.

Born:
May 8, 1884
Lamar, Missouri

Died:
Dec 26, 1972
Kansas City, Missouri
of heart disease

STRANGE & FASCINATING FACTS

He's the only 20th century president who didn't go to college.

The S in his name didn't stand for anything.

He married his childhood friend, Elizabeth or Bess.

He once owned a failing clothing store.

He once worked as a railroad timekeeper.

"It is amazing what you can accomplish if you do not care who gets the credit."
- Harry S Truman

Thirty-Third US President
Of Terms: 1 Partial + 1 Full
Party: Democrat

DWIGHT D EISENHOWER

34TH

1953 to 1961

HOW HE'S REMEMBERED

Eisenhower introduced the beginning of the interstate highway system, which now connects the country.

He ended segregation in schools.

Before serving his two terms as president, he was the supreme commander of the Allied Forces during World War II.

Born:
Oct 14, 1890
Denison, Texas

Died:
Mar 28, 1969
Washington, DC
of heart failure

STRANGE & FASCINATING FACTS

He was the first president to ride in a helicopter.

He got rid of the White House lawn squirrels, which were trapped and released in a nearby park.

He and his five brothers all had the nickname Ike.

He planned the invasion of Normandy, known as D-Day.

Growing up, he worked at the local creamery.

"Pessimism never won any battle."
- Dwight D Eisenhower

Thirty-Fourth US President
Of Terms: 2
Party: Republican

35TH

JOHN F KENNEDY

1961 to 1963

HOW HE'S REMEMBERED

Kennedy won the election via the first televised presidential debates.

He tried but failed to overthrow Cuba's communist leader, Fidel Castro, in what's known as The Bay of Pigs.

He presided over the Vietnam War and the Civil Rights Movement.

Born:
May 29, 1917
Brookline, Massachusetts

Died:
Nov 22, 1963
Dallas, Texas
of a gunshot wound

STRANGE & FASCINATING FACTS

His dad gave him $1 million on his 21st birthday.

Despite a bad recommendation letter claiming Kennedy lacked application and was careless, he still got into Harvard.

Sadly, he was shot and killed while riding in a convertible.

He was obsessed with his weight and traveled with a bathroom scale.

"Efforts and courage are not enough without purpose and direction."
- John F Kennedy

Thirty-Fifth US President
Of Terms: 1 Partial
Party: Democrat

36TH LYNDON B JOHNSON

1963 to 1969

HOW HE'S REMEMBERED

Johnson championed civil rights by signing the Civil Rights Act of 1964 and the Voting Rights Act.

He nominated the first black Supreme Court Justice.

He passed laws to help fight crime and poverty and to protect the environment.

Born:
Aug 27, 1908
Gillespie County, Texas

Died:
Jan 22, 1973
near Stonewall, Gillespie County, Texas
of heart disease

STRANGE & FASCINATING FACTS

He avoided dying in a plane crash because he stopped for a bathroom break at the airport and missed the flight.

He once had a job as a school janitor.

His wife was nicknamed Lady Bird.

He once coached a boy's baseball team.

He was the 2nd tallest president.

"Yesterday is not ours to recover, but tomorrow is ours to win or lose."
- Lyndon B Johnson

Thirty-Sixth US President
Of Terms: 1 Partial + 1 Full
Party: Democrat

RICHARD NIXON
37TH

1969 to 1974

HOW HE'S REMEMBERED

Nicknamed Tricky Dick, he's often remembered for his crimes and corruption, for which he faced impeachment.

However, he did do some good. He established the Environmental Protection Agency.

He also presided over America's moon landing.

Born:
Jan 9, 1913
Yorba Linda, California

Died:
Apr 22, 1994
New York, New York
of a stroke

He played five musical instruments: piano, clarinet, saxophone, violin, and accordion.

After the Watergate Scandal (involving a break-in at the Democratic Headquarters) he resigned to avoid being impeached.

He hosted the largest dinner ever at the White House to welcome home American Vietnam POWs (prisoners of war).

"Remember, always give your best. Never get discouraged. Never be petty."
- Richard Nixon

Thirty-Seventh US President
Of Terms: 1 Full + 1 Partial
Party: Republican

38TH GERALD FORD

1974 to 1977

HOW HE'S REMEMBERED

Ford was both US president and vice president but was never elected to either office!

He ended US involvement in the Vietnam War.

He created treaties with Russia to reduce nuclear weapons.

He pardoned Richard Nixon.

Born:
Jul 14, 1913
Omaha, Nebraska

Died:
Dec 26, 2006
Rancho Mirage, California
of heart disease

STRANGE & FASCINATING FACTS

At college, Gerald Ford was a football star and turned down offers to play on two professional football teams.

During World War II, a typhoon hit his aircraft carrier and caused a fire that nearly killed him.

The University of Michigan retired his football jersey number 48 to honor him.

He's the only president to earn an Eagle Scout badge.

"Never be satisfied with less than your very best effort. If you strive for the top and miss, you'll still beat the pack."
- Gerald Ford

Thirty-Eighth US President
Of Terms: 1 Partial
Party: Republican

JIMMY CARTER
39TH

1977 to 1981

HOW HE'S REMEMBERED

Jimmy Carter created the Department of Education and the Department of Energy.

He tried to negotiate with Iran for the release of 52 US hostages for over a year but failed.

A humanitarian, he founded Habitat for Humanity and won a Nobel Peace Prize.

STRANGE & FASCINATING FACTS

He likes to collect bottles and arrowheads.

He's the first and only president to report a UFO sighting.

His nickname was Hot.

As a kid, he got in big trouble for shooting his sister in the rear end with a BB gun.

A speed-reader, he can read up to 2,000 words a minute.

Born:
Oct 1, 1924
Plains, Georgia

"You can do what you have to do, and sometimes you can do it even better than you think you can."
- Jimmy Carter

Thirty-Ninth US President
Of Terms: 1
Party: Democrat

RONALD REAGAN

40TH

1981 to 1989

HOW HE'S REMEMBERED

He presided over the Cold War and urged Russia to tear down the Berlin Wall.

He created 'Reaganomics', an effort to create more jobs and get the failing economy moving again. It worked.

He acted in over 50 Hollywood movies before his presidency.

Born:
Feb 6, 1911
Tampico, Illinois

Died:
June 5, 2004
Los Angeles, California of Alzheimer's and pneumonia

STRANGE & FASCINATING FACTS

He used an astrologer to organize his schedule.

In 1981 an assassin shot him and he joked, "I forgot to duck".

He was a famous actor but was upset that he never won an Oscar.

He was nearly killed by a chimpanzee.

He was an FBI informant.

He loved jelly beans.

"Heroes may not be braver than anyone else. They're just braver five minutes longer."
- Ronald Reagan

Fortieth US President
Of Terms: 2
Party: Republican

GEORGE BUSH
41ST

1989 to 1993

HOW HE'S REMEMBERED

Bush presided over the Persian Gulf War against Saddam Hussein.

He signed the Americans with Disabilities Act that protects peoples' civil rights.

During the US war on drugs, Panama was Invaded. Their leader, Manuel Noriega, was captured and put on trial.

Born:
Jun 12, 1924
Milton, Massachusetts

Died:
Nov 30, 2018
Houston, Texas
of Parkinson's disease

STRANGE & FASCINATING FACTS

He celebrated his 90th birthday by skydiving.

He and his wife Barbara were the longest-married presidential couple.

While flying in the Navy, he survived being shot down during a bombing run near Japan.

He was knighted by Queen Elizabeth II.

His son was the 43rd president.

"No problem of human making is too great to be overcome by human ingenuity, human energy, and the untiring hope of the human spirit."
- George Bush

Forty-First US President

Of Terms: 1

Party: Republican

42ND BILL CLINTON

1993 to 2001

HOW HE'S REMEMBERED

Clinton presided over the longest period of peacetime economic expansion in American history.

He signed the North American Free Trade Agreement.

He was impeached while president because he lied about something he didn't want people to know about.

Born:
Aug 19, 1946
Hope, Arkansas

STRANGE & FASCINATING FACTS

Clinton won two Grammys for Best Spoken Word Album.

He had a cat named Socks at the White House, but is allergic to cats.

As a kid, he was nicknamed Bubba.

In high-school he played in a band called Three Blind Mice.

His wife, Hillary Rodham Clinton, ran for president against Donald Trump. She won the popular vote, but lost the electoral college vote.

"If you live long enough, you'll make mistakes. But if you learn from them, you'll be a better person."
- Bill Clinton

Forty-Second US President
Of Terms: 2
Party: Democrat

GEORGE W BUSH

43RD

2001 to 2009

HOW HE'S REMEMBERED

He was president during the 9/11 terror attacks, in which a group called Al-Qaeda hijacked airplanes and brought down the Twin Towers in New York City. They flew a third plane into the Pentagon.

He declared global war on terrorism and ordered the invasion of Afghanistan.

STRANGE & FASCINATING FACTS

He was head cheerleader in high school.

As a student at Yale University, he was arrested for stealing a Christmas wreath from a hotel, but the charges were later dropped.

He once owned the Texas Rangers baseball franchise.

His father, George Bush, was the forty-first president.

He was nearly assassinated.

Born:
Jul 6, 1946
New Haven, Connecticut

"A leader is someone who brings people together."
- George W Bush

Forty-Third US President
Of Terms: 2
Party: Republican

BARACK OBAMA

44TH

2009 to 2017

HOW HE'S REMEMBERED

Barack Obama is America's first black president.

He signed the Hate Crimes Prevention Act.

He reformed healthcare to help provide aid to all Americans.

He inherited the Iraq and Afghanistan wars.

He won a Nobel Peace Prize.

STRANGE & FASCINATING FACTS

At school, his nickname was O'Bomber because he was a great basketball player.

He has read every Harry Potter book.

He stopped liking ice cream after his first job scooping it at a Baskin-Robbins store.

He owns a set of boxing gloves autographed by Muhammad Ali.

He grew up in Hawaii.

Born:
Aug 4, 1961
Honolulu, Hawaii

"Change will not come if we wait for some other person or some other time. We are the ones we've been waiting for. We are the change that we seek."
- Barack Obama

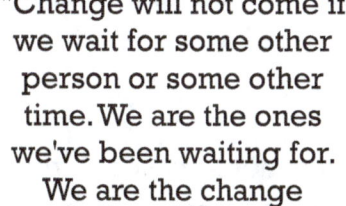

Forty-Fourth US President

Of Terms: 2

Party: Democrat

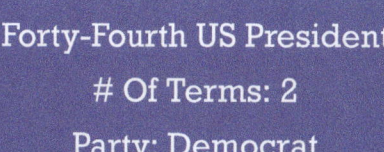

DONALD TRUMP
45TH
2017 to Present

HOW HE'S REMEMBERED

He triggered a trade war with China.

He initiated the Space Force, the 6th branch of the Armed Forces.

He's the third president to be impeached.

As of this writing, he's presiding over the COVID-19 pandemic.

STRANGE & FASCINATING FACTS

He was a television reality star.

As a kid, he was sent to military school due to bad behavior.

He learned to wheel-and-deal from his real-estate salesman dad.

He played a cameo in the movie Home Alone 2.

Born:
Jun 14, 1946
New York, New York

"Without passion you don't have energy, without energy you have nothing."
- Donald Trump

Forty-Fifth US President
Of Terms: Serving 1st
Party: Republican

45

Do you love word search puzzles?

Be sure to check out this fun activity book:

CLEVER KIDS WORD SEARCH
United States Presidents
by Scott Peters

Each beautifully laid out, **large-print** word search puzzle includes **key facts, names, and places** based on the president's fascinating trivia.

AVAILABLE WHEREVER BOOKS ARE SOLD

If you purchased this book without a cover, you should be aware this is stolen property. It was reported as "stripped and destroyed" to the publisher, and neither the author nor the publisher has received any payment for this "stripped book."

Meet America's Presidents: 2-Minute Visits

Copyright © 2020 by Scott Peters and Susan Wyshynski

All rights reserved.

No part of this book may be reproduced in any form or by any electronic or mechanical means, including information storage and retrieval systems, without written permission from the author, except for the use of brief quotations in a book review and as allowed per US Copyright "fair use".

Fair use includes but is not limited to: nonprofit education, which allows teachers to reproduce and distribute copies for classroom use, provided that the amount copied is tailored to include only what is appropriate for the instructor's specific educational goals.

Paperback ISBN: 978-1-951019-15-0

Limit of Liability/Disclaimer of Warranty: This publication is designed to provide accurate and authoritative information in regard to the subject matter covered. While the publisher and author have used their best efforts in preparing this book, they make no representations or warranties with respect to the accuracy or completeness of the contents of this book and specifically disclaim any implied warranties of fitness for a particular purpose.

Cover design by Susan Wyshynski

Illustrations: Kidaha from Pixabay, Antoniosantosg, Yusuf Demirci,

Best Day Books For Young Readers

www.ingramcontent.com/pod-product-compliance
Lightning Source LLC
Chambersburg PA
CBHW081758100526
44592CB00015B/2480